Tequila's Bad Advice
Poetry with the Worm

Collected Poems

by
Judge Santiago Burdon

Tequila's Bad Advice
Poetry with the Worm

Collected Poems

by Judge Santiago Burdon

Tequila's Bad Advice
Poetry with the Worm

By Judge Santiago Burdon

First Edition

Content Copyright © 2023 by Judge Santiago Burdon

All rights reserved.

Author: Judge Santiago Burdon
Editor: Paul Gilliland
Formatting: Southern Arizona Press
Cover Artwork: Traditional Mexican Folk Art, c.1920.

Published by Southern Arizona Press
Sierra Vista, Arizona 85635
www.SouthernArizonaPress.com

ISBN: 978-1-960038-16-6

Poetry

Foreword

The Remnant Leaf Journal

"Judge Santiago Burdon's poetry is a sophisticated slap in the face. The imagery induces you to clear your throat and shift your weight from one side to the other. Judge doesn't waste his words in an attempt to make you comfortable. As a poet he delivers defined grit and structured devastation. He speaks in the language of gasoline fumes and stale cigarette smoke. Always honest and fearless, never apologizing. Know that I am a fan."

S.L. Fleurimont Editor
The Remnant Leaf Journal

Dedication

The addicts, the alcoholics, the homeless and hopeless and all members of the Street Legion, You are not forgotten.

JSB

Contents

Who I Am

I'm a recovering Catholic
drug fiend, and addict,
a drunk, a thief, and ex-con,
musician, writer, half-assed poet, and fighter,
a drifter, failed husband and father,
horrible dancer, a gourmet cook,
Atheist, well-read scholar,
quick tempered, and dog person,
sports fan, a crack shot,
romantic and excellent driver,
A dreamer, jokester, gambler,
and friendly,
punctual, lazy, afraid of spiders,
worked as a smuggler,
too old now to do time,
It's the reason I've retired.

Birth of Santiago

A somber ambience filled the hospital room
on that new moon morning.
He was the fourth son born into a family,
with a mother desperately wanting a girl.
There was no celebration,
no congratulations,
just apologies and sad faces
due to the birth of another boy.

Greeting cards had personal messages written
    inside.
Each person expressing their condolences,
although mentioning they were sure she'd have a
    girl next time.
His parents,
sure they'd be blessed with a daughter,
never considered a name for a boy.

For almost an entire week
the Birth Certificate was left incomplete.
His grandmother made the decision
on what he would be called.
She gave him the same name as her grandfather,
it was also the name of a Saint.
She called him Santiago,
signifying courage, wisdom, and strength.
His father decided the boy would study law.
He added Judge to his name,
although he never imagined his son
would end up appearing in front of so many.

Santiago was baptized with Scotch,
spilled from his Godfather's flask.
Some guests left before the ceremony started
due to the priest arriving late.
He was a constant reminder
of his mother's unanswered prayer.
Another son when she already had three others.
She was a good Catholic woman,
it hardly seemed fair.
Convinced she was being punished.
Knowing Santiago wasn't to blame
she prayed night and day.
Lit candles at church
but something always extinguished the flame.

Four years later she received her reward.
The birth of a daughter.
A gift from the Lord.
In the years that followed as the siblings matured
it was obvious which child the mother preferred.
His sister received most of her parents attention.
He never became jealous or felt ignored.
Seldom did Santiago's activities
come into question.
Their apathy he considered a blessing
In the sparse light of his sister's shadow
he grew into a young man
bound for adventurous mayhem
at the mercy of fate's left hand.

Marty Was A Jew

When I was a kid,
I got invited to my buddy Marty's Bar Mitzvah,
it was for his thirteenth birthday,
his parents were throwing him a big party,
to celebrate a rite of passage.
Ya see, Marty was a Jew.

I told my parents,
I was so excited,
the Bar Mitzvah was at Shedd's Aquarium
    Downtown,
my Old Man said he didn't care,
if it was at fucking Disneyland,
I wasn't going,
and forget about being friends with Marty,
he didn't want him hanging around.
Ya see, Marty was a Jew.

I was more than disappointed,
I was righteously pissed off,
the only reason he had for not letting me go
was because of his religion.
Ya see, Marty was a Jew.

His family didn't seem to mind
that I was a Christian,
you're telling me that's why I can't go,
what's so bad about being a Jew,
my mother put in her two cents worth,
did you know Jews don't believe in Jesus,

what does that have to do with anything,
why does it matter,
maybe Jews don't believe in Bigfoot,
it's not a logical reason.
I knew somehow, in some way,
Jesus would get involved,
why in the hell would Jesus care
if Marty was a Jew,

and there's more pressing world issues
Jesus should be attending to,
hold on here just one minute,
you both have your facts mixed up,
 you don't want me to be friends with Marty
or go to his Bar Mitzvah,
just because of who he doesn't worship.
Marty is a Jew

Yet we go to church every Sunday,
except the Old Man,
and pray to Jesus,
who died on the cross for our sins,
and both of you should be grateful he did,
because what I'm about to say,
you may find hard to believe, I
 guess you forgot this Messiah named Jesus,
or maybe you just never knew,
I read it in the Bible, so I'm sure it must be true,
ya see, Jesus just like Marty,
was a Jew.

No Place To Turn Around

I could have done this
But I went and did that
Had a chance to keep my mouth shut
Needed to say what I said
Went out and challenged fate
When I should have stayed in bed
If I had a chance to do it all over
I'd do the same damn thing again
I try to fool my consciousness into believing.
I'm a victim of circumstance.
I promise to travel a different highway
Knowing there's not a chance.
Because this road to ruin I'm on
Has no place to turn around
No exits, no rest stops, no roadside attractions
My life running on fumes
The fuel gauge on empty

Renegade's Rhapsody

We finally made it to Phoenix.
Johnny's singing in the shower.
We've been waiting for hours
to take care of business.
Spitting out miles of chewed up road.
Contraband couriers of another load.
Now our contact doesn't answer the phone.
Another night in a cheap motel.
Here I am again lying to myself,
promised to quit this business,
but I had my fingers crossed.
No rain since Culiacan
and my mom is probably wonderin'
where her son's off thunderin' to now.
This work costs more than it pays.
Pissed away every dollar I made
and wore a hole in the pocket of my future.
Johnny's dressed just as the telephone rings.
The voice on the line says,
"Gila Casino, Queens Creek."
One more last time we've beat the Devil.
It's because we cheat.

Size Matters

She was a gorgeous girl I met years ago
at Black's Beach near San Diego.
It's a nude beach,
so, I wasn't wearing clothes.
She sat down next to me, then disrobed.
Her body was exquisite
I couldn't help but stare.
She knew I was checking her out
but didn't seem to care.
Soon our conversation turned to sex.
She had a foot fetish.
Thought it was important I knew.
After she inspected my package,
with a disappointed expression she said,
"I guess eight inches will do."

Two 4 One

Saw an advertisement for 2 for 1 today,
I think there must be something wrong with the
     product,
if they need to give one away,
I took advantage of the offer
once I think in Rio de Janeiro,
Some prostitutes offered me 2 for 1,
and I enjoyed having sex in stereo.

The Last Resort

When it gets like this it always comes to that.
I'm left with only one option.
There's always a vacancy at the Last Resort.
No need to make a reservation.
Home to self-loathing and misery.
The only remedy is a lethal cure
All the comforts of self-destruction,
Anguish, and torment are inclusive there
All I've done with my life
is serve my obsessions.
I'm the only thing that stands in my way.
One more screw up
and I'll own the whole collection.
I've learned to swallow the taste of shame.
I poured my heart out, but I guess some spilled.
Now that'll leave a stain.
Like an awful memory that can't be forgotten.
When someone mentions your name.
No credit, no refunds at the Last Resort.
You pay with your blood and tears,
Apologies invalid, promises void,
Excuses told to a deaf ear.
No cocktail lounge to drown your sorrows.
No chapel to kneel down in prayer
No sympathy on the menu
at the Last Resort.
If that's what you're looking for
find somebody who cares.

She Threw A Mean Tarot

Persuaded by a gypsy imposter
to have my Tarot read.
She told me a couple cards were missing
from her Tarot deck
Hoped I didn't mind.
She hadn't taken the time
to figure out which ones yet.
I said it wasn't important,
it's all bullshit anyway.
I don't believe anyone can tell the future.
But I'd play along with her game.
Seven cards were laid out
in a horseshoe pattern.
She told me to think of a question.
Then turned the cards over one at a time.
Her face changed to a serious expression.
She saw an event in my future
that would convince me into believing,
although two cards were missing
from her Tarot deck,
I would still have to pay for the reading.

Angry Streets

The streets are angry tonight.
Traffic unaware of the punishment it inflicts
driving upon their asphalt backs.
Sidewalks click clack with a chaotic rhythm,
footsteps tapping out a nervous pulse,
the throbbing heartbeat of a city near cardiac
    arrest.
Neon lights grow brighter
as night drips darkness
into a black ocean sky.
Overgrown foliage hides a concrete park bench,
my slumber berth for the night.
The cement mattress is harder than I remember.
No reason to complain.
Time to pursue an evasive sleep,
knowing the catch isn't worth the chase.
Left only to wrestle treacherous dreams.
The author of a broken rest.
Car horns, gunfire, and screams
bleed through a chorus of lacerated voices.
Between brief moments of silence
sneaks the moan of a lonely saxophone,
crying notes to a tune I've never heard before,
although it sounds strangely familiar.

Temporary Sherry

The diamond in her wedding ring
has lost its glimmer.
Gone is the sparkle
that once danced in her eyes.
Left with a basket full of laundry.
Every memory a thief
that has robbed her smile.
A hostage of irresistible misfortune,
she keeps telling herself
it's a bad dream.
The sink full of dirty dishes,
her laughter trapped in a scream.
She stares out the kitchen window
sees a future of muffled thunder in broken skies.
Her conversation with silence disrupted
from the sound of the baby's demanding cry.

Face of a New Moon on a Sunlit Night

We walk together arm in arm,
her head resting on my shoulder.
The Sun decides to call it a day,
permitting the night to spill darkness
into a jealous sky,
now pouting because clouds
bullied their way into the vacant space
left by the sun's retreat,
obscuring the brilliant sparkle
of the heavenly stars.

The Earth turns,
introducing the moon beams of soft light.
The scent of magnolia blossoms
travel on every breeze,
the sweet gum and oak trees
appear taller and seem to scratch the sky
with their fingered branches.
The light from streetlamps
dances on her brown skin,
highlighting the minute,
almost invisible,
hairs on her arms.
Her hair smells of lavender
and her skin is soft
like the fur of a sable.
There's a celestial angelic air in her smile,
with an irresistible hypnotic charm in her eyes,

and when I gaze into them,
it's as though she has cast a spell.
In a trance
I drift off to a place
where the night comes to rest,
the stars go to dream,
and the dawn tucks in the Moon.

What Makes Her Beautiful

Even after all the years we've been together,
she still blushes,
unable to hide her embarrassment
whenever I mention how beautiful she is.

My compliment,
always sincere,
somehow makes her feel uncomfortable.

As long as I've known her,
she has never felt comfortable with her beauty.

She doesn't realize
that's something which makes her
all the more beautiful.

Saccharine Kiss

Your Saccharine kiss
only implies the sweetness
that once flavored my lips
with the taste of passion.
Gone is the warmth,
the essence in your touch,
a stinging thorn in moonlight,
the scratch of night's chill.
The brilliance in your eyes
with the reflection of desire
once filled with drifting snowflakes
melted away by the loathing
in your summer sun.
The wonder of your smile,
a contagious pleasure of expression,
now infected by a virus of nefarious color
painting a waterfall,
not spilling a drop.
Your image,
created with seduction
found in clouds.
Now they rain with a precipitation
I no longer recognize.

Black Moon Promise

Bathroom confessions,
backdoor redemption,
black moon promise
made to a leather winged Angel.
Afterglow addict,
disciple of dawn,
woman standing at the edge of love
listening for the silence
in between the words
whispered by an ambidextrous tongue.
Loiterer in dim luminescence
under bloodshot skies.
beautiful visions reminding her
of horrible things
knowing the best part of truth are the lies,
casualty of kindness,
twilight apostle
feeling what is not her favorite color.
A song of flawed perfection
The taste bitter on her lips
Its melody fading
Along with the last smile of summer.

Judge Santiago Burdon

Lesbians Just Don't Like Me

I can't figure it out,
but it's the way it is.
Lesbians just don't like me.
I don't know the reason why.
I've been told I have that look,
whatever the hell that means.
Maybe it's the mustache.
Don't think I have bad breath.
I'm sure it's not body odor.
Maybe they've mistaken me
for some other guy.
It's beginning to hurt my feelings,
I'd like to know why.
When I offer a cordial smile,
they stare with disgusted expressions.
Some stick out their tongue
or give me the finger.
Why am I treated with such aggression?
I've asked what it is about me
that causes such disdain.
They yell, "leave us alone, dumbass breeder.
Get the fuck away."
I was beat up by some lesbians
one time when I was shit faced drunk.
I think it was in Madison, Wisconsin.
I don't have a clue why I was jumped.
They broke my nose
and gave me a black eye.
One kept trying to kick me in the balls.
When it was over,

one of them pulled down her pants
and pissed on me
while I was passed out on the floor.
I've never criticized their lifestyle.
I don't care who anyone fucks.
Everyone should have the same opportunity
to choose who to date or love.
It's a question that will never be answered.
I guess it will always be a mystery.
I'll go to my grave without knowing,
"Why lesbians just don't like me."

An Addict's Lament

I'll just have to start over.
After ten months of being sober
my weakness proved to be stronger
than my determination to stay clean.
Searched for a valid reason to get high.
That didn't sound like an excuse;
resulted in a list of lies.
I used to bribe the truth.
I deserved a reward
for all the progress I'd made.

Listen to me
trying to justify my actions
for what I had just thrown away.
I'll blame my sponsor,
say it's all his fault
for being out of town.
When I needed his help most
he wasn't around.

Temptation befriended me
encouraging my decision.
Where the hell is it now
that I've become guilt ridden?
What am I thinking,
who's gonna know
that I relapsed and got high
unless I tell them so?

I can live with the lie.
Big deal, it's not the first time.
After all, I'm just a junkie and addict
fighting a losing battle
with my habit.

Sugar Mama

I need a sugar mama,
someone to take care of me.
Let me drink in the bar,
drive her Porsche car,
watch her big screen TV

When my pockets don't jingle
she'll always spare a couple of bucks.
She'll never ask where I've been
but when I do come in
she can always count on my love
as long as her checks don't bounce.

She doesn't have to be pretty,
beauty's nothing money can't buy.
I can picture me in her Jacuzzi
living the easy life.

Say I'm a fool for money.
I've been a bigger fool for love.
Why should I give it away
when I can make it pay
and enjoy working overtime,
not worried about nickels and dimes

I need me a sugar momma
To take me under her wing.
I'll kiss her hand,
I'll say yes ma'am,
won't curse in front of her friends.
We'll vacation down in Barbados
getting suntanned on her yacht
with a beer in my hand

I'll think of my friends
and everything they ain't got.
I'll be happy
believe it or not.

Sugar Mama,
I'll do just what I'm told.
Sugar Mama,
I'll be your country boy gigolo.
I'll throw away my boots and jeans,
shave and wear a Tuxedo.
Even learn the Tango
and teach you how to Cotton Eye Joe.

Sugar Mama
take me home.

Judas Was Framed

Judas was framed.
I was the one, it was me.
I gave him the thirty pieces of silver.
I lost a bet we had made
over whether or not he would kiss
some long-haired Jewish carpenter.

They were all getting drunk
at some religious-type event,
maybe it was a Bingo game.
It took a few glasses of wine
for him to work up the nerve.
He finally gave him a kiss.
He won the bet fair and square.

Romans arrested the Jewish carpenter.
He was charged with quite a few crimes:
Claimed he was a bootlegger
who could turn water into wine,
practiced medicine without a license,
brought the dead back to life.
He even restored sight to the blind.
He had an amazing trick
that made it appear
as though he could walk on water.

It's said with a single loaf of bread
he fed thousands.
One hell of a fisherman,
charged with poaching,
catching over the limit.
He was no son of god,
only a magician
with a few very good tricks and gimmicks.
The sheriff Ponty Pilot
gave him a strict sentence.
They're going to nail him to a cross.
The Jews bought the lumber
as well as the nails.
I'm told that they got it all at cost.
There will be a huge celebration,
the day of the execution,
Good Friday is the theme for the event.
The Romans sure know how
to make a crucifixion fun.
For the cost of your admission
they're going to crucify two others.
That's three for the price of one.

Judas is accused of being a snitch.
There's no proof,
although he's still under suspicion.
They point their fingers
and bear false witness.
Screaming insults at him in public.
Isn't that just like a Christian.

Legend of Fosse Way

Riding hard under a moonlight high
not a leaf rustling, it troubles my mind
In the distance, I hear music of the lyre and flute
The melody serenading the stars
The voice of a maiden
bleeds its way through the darkness
singing an ole bawdy Pub Song
My steed swift at a gallop
hooves sound their click clack
crossing Halford Bridge we press on

History demands I deliver this message
I must make Exeter Castle by dawn
Two Queens vie for the throne of England
Not even God can decide which is the virtuous one

Forest fairies ring the bells on the Foxglove
The Oaks without expression and still
A rare breeze slaps awake sleeping grass in the
      glades
toads croak their complaint to the night's chill
This road is dominion of highwaymen and thieves
Robbing those that choose this way to travel
By the will of My Lord and with the Bishop's
      blessing
I will pass undetected by scoundrels and rabble.

Nourished on only bread and Brambleberries
Traveling by night taking sleep by day
All that I've seen are ghosts of Roman soldiers
On this road known as Fosse Way
Say my name Trevor Harrison be mentioned
in yarns told about pubs and taverns
History will decide if I be 'Patriot or Traitor'
As a result of my actions.
My only wish is not to be forgotten
And live on in memory of this day
As one of the many legends
the many legends of Fosse Way.
In memory of my distant relative
Robert Devereux, 2nd Earl of Essex.

Jalopy

Junkyard treasure
discovered under a pile of worn tires
held together with bailing wire,
duct tape, and faith.

Antique veteran of time
traveled back roads,
long before miles of Interstate Highway were laid,
you still refusing to retire.

Land yacht Titanic,
once admired by wanting eyes,
viewed now with smug glares
seeing only wounds of wear,
unseen are years of loyal service.

Opulent commander of all roads,
now surrendering the right of way,
to compacts and sports cars
with reputations of low gas mileage performance.

Pile of sun-tortured rusted metal
past resurrection of a Simoniz massage,
unable to restore the brilliance you shined,
when your paint glimmered with color.

Your perseverance was rewarded
with my grin of appreciation,
everytime I turned the key in your ignition,
sparking life into your forever engine,
that delivered me to another destination.

Jalopy my first car,
you introduced me to street freedom.
My magic carpet
with four bald tires
and three on the tree,
the ride I'd drive
with pride in my youth.

We journeyed countless
teenage smiling miles together,
never will I forget the open roads,
flying with a speed that beat the racing wind

cruisin'
just me and you
cruisin'
just me and you.

How I Remember That Day

I remember the Sunday you burst onto the scene
in your typical dramatic fashion.
Your entrance so hurried you were so impatient
a characteristic you still possess
My Raiders were playing for a spot in the playoffs
Two reasons for me to be excited on that day
Alone with your mother
She was laboring not to give birth
Planned for you to be born at home
But you wouldn't wait
for the midwife to arrive
so, you bullied, pushed and forced your way out
into this world
but you didn't cry
Raiders first and goal at the nine-yard line
when I first saw your face you smiled at me
I was impressed by you being so calm
your mother worried by your serene demeanor
Had me check to be sure you were breathing
Incomplete pass, second and goal
Kindness in your grin
And a keen perception in your eyes
I counted ten fingers, ten toes.
You were physically fine

Next I tied the umbilical cord
Holding my breath I cut.
You took hold of my thumb
And squeezed tight
Raiders with no time outs
Fourth and goal
Just then the midwife arrived
quickly she checked on you and your mother
Reporting you both were fine.
She asked how I was doing
I said I wasn't feeling well at the time.
What's wrong with you she questioned
My Raiders just lost the football game
I noticed a bit of scorn in her eyes
Despite the Raider's loss your birthday was epic
It's how I remember the day.
You've grown into a man of certain distinction
As I look at you now
I'm beyond impressed
how proud I am that you're my son
Causing a need for me to express
I'm amazed by the man you've become
Also the fact you're a Raiders fan
Happy birthday.
I love you Gentry.
And one last thing I must convey:
No having fun today

Wheel Man

This run is my swan song,
after tonight this smugglings gonna stop,
every headlight in my rearview mirror,
looks like it's a cop,
all these kilos in back,
they're weighing heavy on my mind,
I can't get busted,
Lord knows, I'm too old to do any more time.

I sleep with one eye open,
I keep the other on my gun,
I'm the only friend I've got,
and I'm not sure,
he's one I can trust,
you think it's easy money,
it costs far more than it's worth,
profit from broken lives,
it's blood stained and cursed.

I run on stolen luck and unheard prayers,
no guarantees in this business,
my insurance is some criminal's word.
I've used so many aliases,
my real name I've forgot,
lost a wife and family,
and too many friends to count.

Don't judge this life of mine,
don't put the blame on me,
I'm just the wheelman bringing you,
you and you with what you need.

Apocalyptic Tattoo

I smoke Rock. I drink Scotch.
I like hookers that don't talk a lot.
I smile from the pain
when the needle tears through my vein.

I don't need Jesus to forgive me.
My salvation would cost more than I can pray.
Absolution can't be purchased
no matter how many Hail Marys you say.

An empty bottle becomes a victim,
another Soldier that I drank to death.
Tiny plastic bags lay empty
While the drug swims in the blood under my flesh.

It would take more than an army of Christian
    Soldiers
on a crusade to save my soul.
A futile quest to rescue an empty spirit
that's been ravaged, robbed, bought, and sold.
In twisted darkness or crooked light
seeking venom from piercing fangs.
The healing cure in a snake's bite.

There's no trust in a junkies smile,
no grief in his tears.
Rusted words from an acid tongue
spit out and insincere.
Fate left no clue, just a bruise
My Apocalyptic Tattoo.
Was I the one that made this choice
or was it this addiction
imitating my voice?

Stone of Nihilism

Stained glass lies.
Colored shards of broken truth.
Puzzle pieces arranged in
sanctimonious expression.
Designed to camouflage falsehoods.
The perjury of Priests.
Disguised deceit in windows
of brilliant rainbow hues
lighted by the sunlight of fraudulent confession.
Hypocrisy designed
with prismatic glass of fragile faith
proudly hang in your Church of Shame.
My single stone of Nihilism
will shatter the pigmented panes
of your tinted atrocities.

Judge Santiago Burdon

God's Funeral

I was the only pallbearer at God's funeral.
I dragged the casket the last twenty-five yards.
They served Deviled Eggs and Devil's Food Cake.
The Christians brought Mogen David wine.

All the deity guests present argued
who should bare the blame
for allowing Nietzsche and Darwin
to spread blasphemous theories
causing worshippers to question their faith.

Jesus couldn't have cared less.
Considered to be a prodigal son
he was busy cheating Catholics at Bingo,
acting like a false prophet
the Jews knew he was.

Shiva eating his T-Bone steak.
Sitting alone at a table
watching Thetans perform the "Space Opera"
Entertainment provided by the Scientology
    Church.

Allah found the play amusing,
saying Xenu had been falsely accused.
Judas commented, "ya tell me about it."
Everyone knows it was you claimed the Jews.

My Kevorkian Alter Ego

This charade is an overplayed drama.
A boring non-event.
The only thing that has died
is my interest.

Stop with the Greek Tragedy:
Cutting your wrists,
Swallowing pills,
Attempted O.D.'s.
Pathetic cries for help.
No one is listening.

It's embarrassing to watch
these acts of a coward.
A gun in your mouth,
a hair trigger.
That's a nice touch.

An electric appliance in the bathtub.
Use a toaster,
makes a great headline "He's Toast!"
These are methods sure to end it.
Your slow boat to death
has run out of rivers.

The Heroin Cocaine Oxys the Meth Condiments
used to flavor your depression.
So, let's get it over with.
Time to make the grand exit.
What makes you think
anyone gives a fuck.
Go ahead and jump.
Make a big splash.
That'll show 'em.
You don't give a fuck either.

Thought I Heard My Mama Call

Walked miles of dead-end dirt road.
Can't shake this feeling
it won't leave me alone.
The breeze laughing at me through the trees,
Thought I heard my mama call.

Wisconsin, born and raised,
corn growing earth running through my veins.
Stars burning holes through the night sky.
I thought I heard my mama call.

Somebody tell me
is there life beyond this town.
I've got a wantin',
I'm sick and tired of hanging 'round.

Country living
somehow lost its charm,
I've grown restless
with life down on the farm.

I need to feel
this town behind me.
I need to go
where they can't find me.

The grass is greener,
but here I'm color blind.
I had a calling.
The wind sang my name on a summer night.
I'm not burning bridges.
I'll always call this place my home.
The time has come for me
to strike out on my own.

I need to dream
without a reason.
I need to be
the one I pleasing.

I sowed these fields
but I never planted roots.
This farm is my daddy's dream
I've got getting' in my boots.

Time to catch up with my future.
Can't let another day slip by.
Packed a smile in my pocket.
Won't leave a memory behind.
I need to know,
what it is that I'm after.
I need to find
what is in life that matters.
I thought I heard my mama call.

Last Laugh

I don't ask for much these days,
a hot meal, a safe place to sleep,
and when I meet my end to go quickly,
with the least amount of pain,
I do beg this favor,
after I've cashed in my chips,
proving my belief in immortality a myth,
place my body in the dumpster,
behind the Burger King on third,
the one near Saint Francis Church,
pin a note to my shirt
with this message in large print,
so, it's easy to read,

"I warned all of you
not to eat food from this dumpster,
I told you it was not only poisonous but deadly,
I've never followed my own advice,
maybe now you'll finally believe me!"

Then I will have had the "Last Laugh."

Give My Best to Wisconsin

Talking with an old friend out in the Southwest.
He felt it was time to be getting on home.
All the crops were ready for harvest.
Said he was tired of life on the road.
He had to get on back there,
had to feel the wind in his hair.
He left her waiting there on him.
With a hard handshake we said goodbye.
I asked buddy if you find the time,
can you do a favor for me,
Give my best to Wisconsin.
Tell her not to wait for me,
I've been lost out in Arizona,
she'll always be home to me.

I left more than friends and family back there.
There's part of me I left behind.
Out of all the places I've been to
Wisconsin has always owned a piece of my heart.
With every breath I breathe,
Wisconsin lives inside of me.
She touched me to my soul.
I pray for the day when once again
we come together like long lost friends.
Will she remember my name?
Give my best to Wisconsin,
tell her not to wait for me,
I've been lost out in Arizona,
she'll always be a dream to me.
Wisconsin will always be home to me.

Here With Me You Will Stay

I lie next to you in the partial darkness
lit only by a single bulb hanging from a wire.
I watch you sleep in a permanent slumber.
Your body, cold with a rigid disdain.
No longer a raging rhythm
pounding in your heart of cruel intention.
Silenced are the words
you shouted to damn me,
leaving you breathless never to voice again.
Conceit reflected in your beauty,
now fading with each ticking moment.
The weight of time we spent together
measured in ounces
never equated to a pound of love.
Your threats of abandonment,
leaving me alone without regret
will never be realized.
Made certain by the keen edged blade of my knife
when I slit your delicate throat.

Dandelions and Dragonflies

Tell me how can it be.
You've become so close to me.
We have yet to gaze
upon each other's face.
Yet I'm a familiar foreigner to your seductive smile
and the suggestive allure
in your temptation eyes.
I'm sure you're not roses and butterflies.
So ordinary and passe.
You admire the elegance in dandelions and
    dragonflies
dancing an allegro in nature's ballet.
There's a sparkle in your loveliness,
its twinkle you choose not to recognize.
You're uncomfortable with the brilliance defining
    your beauty
which makes you more beautiful than you realize.
Your favorite flavor is summer,
the same as mine.
You choose the wind as the color
to decorate the truth in your lies.
In your touch, a kindness reaching deep into my
    soul.
Your heart a treasure.
Wealthy the man who finds the key
to open the treasure chest
you've kept closed.

Don't Ask My Advice

I don't give advice.
So don't ask for mine.
I'm just an old man.
My age doesn't make me wise.
There's no volumes of worldly knowledge
or Cosmic revelation
I've acquired over time
of scholarly information.
You want to know why
I don't give advice?
Listen up and I'll explain:
If you give advice
and it results in failure,
the person who received it
now has "**You**"
to blame.

Judge Santiago Burdon

My Kind of Woman

I want a woman
with the faint taste of cocaine on her lips,
a dash of peril in her kiss,
with laughter that sings
like mission bells at midnight,
a cool summer breeze in her touch,
the smell of a far-off rain in her hair,
her skin smooth as a river stone,
there's temptation in her smile,
a hint of confession in her lies,
enticement on her breath,
green ocean waves splash in her eyes,
and she can throw a mean punch.

It's When I Think of You

Walking through the city streets late at night,
the rain soaking me to the bone.
It's on rainy nights like this
when I think of you most.
It makes me want to come by your home
to tell you something that happened
a long time ago
when we parted and went our separate ways.
Please don't think I'm accusing you
of being a kleptomaniac,
but you took my Repel Umbrella
and I want it back!

Judge Santiago Burdon

Buttered Side Down

That's when I knew
she no longer loved me.
Not like she did before.
She thought it would go by unnoticed.
But I saw what she did with the toast
that fell on the kitchen floor.

She was quick with the pickup
and didn't think twice
about putting it on my plate.
What I didn't know wouldn't hurt me.
I'd never be able to tell by the taste.

I'm not going to say anything about it,
she'd just get defensive and pissed off.
Screaming at me that's not how it happened
then somehow making it all my fault.

I wasn't going to eat the piece of toast
and give her the satisfaction
to think she pulled one over on me.
So, I put my plan into action.

I dropped the toast
making it look like an accident.
It landed buttered side down
on the kitchen floor.
She didn't say a word
just kept eating her eggs
the incident went by ignored

I went into the kitchen
to make another.
She said as I looked for the bread,
she used the last slice
there wasn't any more.
If I wanted another piece of toast
I'd have to go to the store.

They Can't Kill Me

They can't kill me.
Although many have tried.
All disappointed by the results
when they discovered I had survived.

The Police and gangsters,
Mexican and Colombian gangs,
and even Drug Dealers
I failed to pay.

Ex-husbands of women,
ex-girlfriends that felt betrayed,
car accidents and a plane crash,
But I walked away.

I've lived through earthquakes,
hurricanes, volcanic eruptions,
even tornadoes
that caused devastating destruction.

I've been bitten by scorpions,
a Brazilian Wandering Spider,
a rattlesnake, and jelly fish -
all painful reminders.

Survived Prostate Cancer,
a Sepsis Infection causing a 30-day coma,
Tuberculosis when I was just a kid,
Two heart attacks, and Double Pneumonia.

Maybe now you'll understand
and may possibly believe,
they can't kill me, I'll never die
due to my immortality.

Rest in Peace, Not Me

When I die,
unless my suspicion of immortality be true,
if I'm fortunate enough to be acknowledged,
I ask that *Rest In Peace* is not mentioned or used.
Such a trite acronym to sum up a life,
It's an accepted excuse
for those with nothing better to say.
A condolence so condescending,
all you were worth was just a three-word cliche.
It's a blessing started in the eighth century by
     Romans,
stolen later by Christians
unable to think of an original phrase.
It's not the first time they've stolen ideas
when creating their religion.
They did the same thing inventing Jesus.

If an afterlife exists
and I'm accepted as a resident,
I'm not spending eternity,
Resting In Peace.
I'm going to smile out loud,
turn up the music,
sing along with the song,
and dance naked in the streets,
Rest In Peace,
Not me!

Judge Santiago Burdon

About the Author

The Odyssey of Judge Santiago Burdon began in the "City of Big Shoulders", as Sandburg called it in his poem "Chicago". He was born during Mayor Richard Daley's first days in office and Eisenhower's first term as President.

His father named him Judge, hoping he would pursue a career in law. He had no idea his son would end up appearing in front of so many.

Santiago attended Universities in the United States and abroad, focusing his studies on Victorian Literature and Authors. His short stories and poems have been featured in over two hundred magazines, on-line literary journals, podcasts, and anthologies. He was recognized in "Who's Who of Emerging Writers 2020" and again in 2021. His first book *Stray Dogs and Deuces Wild Cautionary Tales* was published in January 2020 by Arthur Graham Editor Horror Sleaze Trash Press. His next book, a collection of poems, *Not Real Poetry* was published in July 2021 by Steve Cawte, Editor of Impspired Press, Lincolnshire, England. Arthur Graham, Editor of Horror Sleaze Trash Press launched Santiago's third book, *Quicksand Highway* with more short stories of expeditions into irresistible bedlam in September 2021. Steve Cawte, Editor/Publisher Impspired Press, published *Fingers In The Fan* the fourth book by Santiago, July 2022. Another collection of short stories with the same gritty dialogue, dark humor and cautionary tales Santiago has popularized in his other books.

Tequila's Bad Advice - Poetry with the Worm, a second collection of visceral poetry is scheduled to be launched March 2023 by Paul Gilliland, Editor/Publisher, Southern Arizona Press. A sixth book by this outlandish author, *Lords Of The Afterglow Renegades and Noblemen* is yet another collection of Bohemian Tales and adventurous mayhem which will also be published by Paul Gilliland, Editor/Publisher of Southern Arizona Press in the summer of 2023.

Santiago turned 69 last July and is living modestly in Costa Rica.

Previous Works

Stray Dogs and Deuces Wild Cautionary Tales (2020)
Not Real Poetry (2021)
Quicksand Highway (2021)
Fingers In The Fan (2022)

www.ingramcontent.com/pod-product-compliance
Lightning Source LLC
Chambersburg PA
CBHW071850020426
42331CB00007B/1937